IT'S A CAT'S LIFE.

Stanley Hemming-Clark

**VERSES with a CAT'S THOUGHTS,
ADVENTURES, PROVERBS,
MISUNDERSTANDINGS
with COMMENTS
on HUMAN NATURE**

Searchline Publishing

Searchline Publishing
Searchline House
Holbrook Lane
Chislehurst
BR7 6PE
www.searchlinepublishing.co.uk

ABOUT THE AUTHOR

The Author read Latin with French, and Theology, at Cambridge. He was Vicar of a Kent Parish for 38 years, combining this with teaching posts. He now lives near Guildford. Serious publications include two books on Theology and *Hymns and Meditations on the Seven Words*. Humorous include many written for "ad hoc" occasions.

First published 2009

ISBN: 978-1-897864-23-4

INTRODUCTION & DEDICATION

Verses showing a cat's thoughts about life and humans, including some Misunderstandings, Adventures, Proverbs and Sayings, with a bit of Philosophy and Psychology, and some Sonnets and Epigrams.

Dedicated to my wife Stella, who wrote the Foreword, and the Memory of the Cats who have shared our life and given ideas for some of these verses – Pinkle Purr, Tattoo, Blackie, Ginger, Polly and the pedigree Blue, Ranshill Ferdinand, known as Dusty.

FOREWORD by Stella Hemming-Clark

The first of these poems is slightly different from the others in its approach. It is based on an experience when a cat suddenly appeared, seeming disorientated. Although we adopted her, she always seemed a little bit wary of close contact. The poem Removal Day imagines what may have lain behind this.

In the other poems we see life and a family through the eyes of the cat. The cat, in whose person the verses are written, hears what humans are saying, but does not always understand. Sometimes there are Proverbs and common Sayings. At times our cat consults Old Tom, a wiser and older cat; Tom is sometimes right, but will never admit that he is not certain - a characteristic of some humans too!

Some verses will be appreciated by those who, for example, have been offered a dead mouse by their cat, or who have tried to give medicine to one.

Our cat even tries his hand at writing Sonnets and Epigrams.

We hope that some of these verses will "ring a bell" with those familiar with a cat's life and attitudes, and give fresh insights to some who are not.

REMOVAL DAY

See foreword. To the cat, using sense images rather than reason, it would seem that the world had somehow changed. In contrast the two families question and reason, but each knows only half of the event. "Curious" in verse 1 is contrasted with "Confused" in verse 5. The sixth verse suggests a parallel with human sense of loss.

"REMOVAL VAN" stood in the road:
Curious, a neighbour's Pussy crept...
The van drove off with well-packed load,
In which the cat curled up and slept.

At last the van came to a stop
About two hundred miles away.
Puss stirred, jumped out with eager hop
And found - her world had gone away.

Back home her owners, much dismayed,
Searched, called her name, then advertised.
"She's stolen, dead, or simply strayed?"
Her end could only be surmised.

Far off some found her lost, discussed -
"Whose is this cat none seems to claim?"
They took her in and won her trust,
Gave her a home and chose a name.

All thought and talked, but never found
What happened on removal day.
Confused, the cat sensed all around
The world she'd known had gone astray.

We rest, curled up in well-loved scenes,
Till loss and grief strike in one day.
Friends talk, use words...We sense it means
The world we loved has slipped away.

THE BURGLARY

This is based upon an actual event. We were burgled more than once, when nobody was in the house except our cat Ranshill Ferdinand, commonly known as Dusty, a British Blue. We often wondered what he thought of the event. This poem imagines his thoughts...

A strange thing happened last Saturday:
I was all alone: they'd gone away.
I'd planned my time - rest, then take a snack...
Walk round the house...think...till They come back.

A ring on the bell, a knock on the door.
Calls such as these I prefer to ignore -
Can't reach the handle without leaping,
Stay in the chair and carry on sleeping.
If it's important they'll come next day:
All is quite still, so they've gone away -
But then
Sudden
Smash!
Crash!
Shatter!
What *is* the
matter??!!
Bump!
Thump!

Through kitchen window on to the floor
(But guests always walk through the front door)
Two men appeared:
One had a beard:
One tall, thin, hair a mess,
Plastic gloves! - but shabby dress,
Shoes a disgrace:
Unfamiliar face:
Hatchet in hand
(I don't understand).

2

They pulled at drawers,
Forced open doors,
Made a big mess
Of all we possess.
"Give that box a bash -
it could have some cash"
"Take that silver, Sid,
will fetch a few quid."
Thumping upstairs,
Moving our chairs.
"Necklace - gold rings -
Take all them things."
"Find a bag, Arry -
That's all I can carry."
Downstairs with a thump:
"Be quick!" Clump: clump!
"Take that stuff -
That's enough."
With no more sound: last look around.

I had just a rough poke,
Not my usual soft stroke

They opened the back door from inside
And hurried through, left open wide:
Took a quick look to left and right
And swiftly vanished out of sight.

"What can this mean?" I asked, alarmed,
But thankful that I'd not been harmed.
Friends often come and sometimes stay
But none of them behave this way.

My people soon returned - Commotion!
Rushed round the house in consternation,
She gave a squeak: He gave a groan
And hurried to the telephone.

The two strange men? I'd guessed it right -
Were not some friends they might invite.
Two men came next, much smarter chaps,
Both dressed in blue, peaks on their caps.
They asked my people what they'd missed,
Wrote lots of notes and made a list.
With something about a "Scene of Crime."
A girl came too and spent some time
Shaking some stuff (What could it mean?)
Where the two strange men had been.
More words were said - "Victim Support" -
Something was wrong, just as I'd thought.

"We'll try our best." said the men in blue:
"Evidence suggests that there were two:
No finger prints but just one clue:
Window sill has the mark of a shoe."

"No-one was here when this took place
To hear a name or see a face".

I WAS. I saw them come and saw them go:
Could tell you all you need to know.
I saw their faces, heard their name:
But cannot tell: it's such a shame.

No-one would listen as they ought
If a Pussy Cat stood up in court.

MAD MOMENTS

At times even the most placid cat will sometimes, quite
unpredictably, have some mad moments...

WE CATS have gained a reputation
For spending hours in contemplation:
Each one sits silent while he thinks
And motionless as any sphinx.
This feline characteristic
Makes each one seem a mystic.
Then suddenly some night or morning
All will change without a warning.

      Psychologists can never find
      Some hidden trauma in our mind:
      No moralist can classify:
      Their usual terms do not apply.
      Not good: not bad: We just GO MAD.

Round and round with a leap and a bound:
Kick long-lost ball from wall to wall
Up and down along the hall:
Rush through each door: Leap from the floor:
Jump on each chair, anywhere, everywhere:
Paper tear, throw in the air, rush up the
stairs in pairs: Hop from the top: suddenly
Stop: Try to fly: Fling anything: Fiercely
attack - whack! Whack the bed! Leave
The Pillow quite quite dead: Another leap -
Clothes for sleep flung in a heap.
Glide, slide, side to side.

This madness past, I am quite sane,
Resume my look of cold disdain.
It's just a thing We Pussies do:
We don't know why, so how would you?

FIVE SENSES

PEOPLE HAVE FIVE SENSES: so They claim,
    And, humanlike, they give each one a name:
Taste, Smell, Hearing, Smelling, Touch.
    Of their first two, I don't think much.

Their sense of Taste
Has gone to waste.
Their sense of smell? -
Has gone as well.

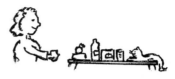

I did some Field Research last Saturday
(She thought I was nosey, getting in Her way).
Sunday I spent in quiet thought:
By Monday was ready to write my Report.

Here it is -
A comparison of the FIVE SENSES between
Homo Sapiens and Feles Domestica with
special Reference to the Olfactory and
Gustatory Senses, including Details of
Methodology and Research, by Pussy Cat Ph.D.

When She comes back from a trip to the shops
First - exhausted - in a chair She flops.
Then all the plastic bags She unpacks -
Jars, Bottles, Tins, Boxes, small sacks.

As She placed each on the table
I carried out Research on the label...

Each one would state
A "Sell by" date
Or "After use, refrigerate"
Or "Use by December 2008"
"Best before the end of May"
"Eat before a such and such day"

6

"Do not freeze this meat again"
"These jars some additives contain"
"This margarine is free from fats"
"This is the Purrfect Food for Cats"
(Oh Yeah?)
"Splendid Value in this tin"
"This food has Extra Vitamin"
"Cook just as the label states"
"This fat contains Unsaturates"
"Gently cook but do not boil"
"All made with healthy Olive Oil"
"Best within five days of buying"
"This is the ideal fat for frying"
"Carefully mix into a batter"
"This food contains no colouring matter"

WE DON'T NEED THIS! We cats can tell
If our food is fit, by our SENSE OF SMELL.
Our SENSE OF TASTE has always told
If milk is even one day old.

If any food is slightly stale
We show it firmly by our tail.
If all's not purrfect with our fish,
We turn our nose up at the dish.
If any meat is slightly poor,
Annoyed, we scratch the wall or floor.
However much they try to tempt,
WE KNOW - and react with contempt.

We don't need printing on the label:
Our SENSE OF TASTE AND SMELL is able
To show at once and without fail
What's good and fresh or bad and stale.

CHRISTMAS DAY

Another thing that shows they're crazed -
I realized and sat amazed
And for a while I simply gazed
    On Christmas Day.

Those strange. odd presents that they gave
Even the calmest start to rave:
In ecstasy their hands they wave
    In a mad way.

Jumpers in a Christmas Box,
Coloured scarves and thermal frocks,
Knitted gloves and woolly socks
    Keep cold away.

We cats don't need such gifts to share,
Or give each other wool to wear:
We grow ourselves some thicker hair
    For wintry day.

Some After Shave whose scent will fade,
Or Shaving Soap and Razor Blade,
Electric razor specially made
    To shave hair away!

In all this Toiletry Range,
The gift that seems most odd and strange -
Dye that will make their colour change
    To black from grey.

Bath foam, bath cubes, shampoos I've seen,
Lotions, gels, soaps yellow, red, green,
All shapes and sizes just to clean
    Their dirt away.

We cats don't need this kind of stuff:
To clean our fur, both soft and rough,
Long careful licks are quite enough
Six times a day.

Some give wine, bottles of booze,
That makes them lose their wits and snooze:
Surely they know? Yet still they choose
Hangovers next day!

And yet the most exciting thing -
The paper and the bits of string,
Boxes, sticky tape - they fling
Quite careless away.

We cats can have a lovely caper
Tearing crinkly wrapping paper,
Patting lights and chewing taper,
Have a great play.

Pull labels and envelopes to bits,
Rolling as if we're throwing fits,
Then jump as if we'd lost our wits
All through the day.

I hide in every box I find,
A ball of string chase and unwind:
Such happiness for feline kind
Whatever people say.

These gifts this cat appreciated!
I've never felt so animated.
But humans when they celebrated
Had such a dull day.

HOLIDAYS: a Lament

In June and July there's no cloud in the sky
    And lassies and lads turn to folly.
I sit all forlorn on the edge of the lawn
    Immersed in a deep melancholy.

Though the days are long and the birds sing their song,
    My heart is heavy with pain:
I feel in my head that what I most dread
    Is creeping round once again.

I watched Their faces and saw their suitcases:
    I sense They're planning to roam.
The word "Holiday" – that's the reason They say
    For leaving me all alone.

I never shall know of the place where they go
    After this planning and packing.
They just disappear at this time of the year
    And half my life is now lacking.

I shan't fade away for They're kind in their way:
    Morning and night I'll be fed.
Good folks come to feed, look to see what I need,
    Make sure I'm ready for bed.

But I can't go In...Out...or wander about:
    No-one will open the door.
I can't freely roam in and out of the home.
    Life's not the same any more.

I miss human voices, even shouting and noises.
    I miss the lap where I sat,
Even the cleaning. Life loses its meaning
    Without hands to stroke or pat.

However I try, I shall never know why
    They have this strange urge to roam:
But all that I know – when my people all go
    They leave me lonely at home.

READING THE NEWS

Most people take a paper every day:
    Mine take the *Telegraph*.
Sometimes the News is grim and grey
    But sometimes makes us laugh.

Pages of Crimes, Wars, Other News,
    Scandal, Gossip and Sports,
Gardening Notes, articles with views,
    Health, and Weather Reports.

WE CATS can read our News as well,
    But don't need yards of print.
We use our eyes and sense of smell,
    Instinct and subtle hint.

I take my place at five to eight
    Upon the window sill:
See Mr. Smith is leaving late -
    They say his wife is ill.

The Postman brings a pile of mail,
    Maybe stops and chatters:
Oh good! The Milkman does not fail
    To bring the drink that matters.

See that pair chat up each other,
    Though she is going grey?
"Old enough to be his mother,"
    I heard my people say.

The kids are having a Football Match,
    So I know it's Saturday.
They're playing on that old waste patch,
    So I know it's Home not Away.

Now is the time to investigate
The various parts of my estate.
Slowly, keen-eyed I march around
To see that all is safe and sound,
To see that all is free from fear
In each outpost of my frontier...

Smell in the air
Shows Fox was there.
We've been raided
And invaded
By next door's cat -
I'll soon fix that:
Realpolitik will do the trick
(A savage glare
With teeth all bare!)
Bough severed here -
Wind was severe.
Hello! New pot
put in this spot.
He's cleared those weeds...
These look like seeds:
This simple thing
Shows it's Spring.
He's dug I see
Beneath that tree:
It will just do
For a Cat's Loo.
Weather report?
My mother taught
Me how to sense
The elements,
So when it pours
I'm safe indoors.

Local Gossip, Crime, Weather, News,
Wars, Hygiene, Nature, Garden, Views...
All the great happenings of my place and age -
I read them all without a printed page.

THE NEW BABY

I thought I knew all forms of life,
     The ones I mostly see-
The husband and his lady wife
     And guests who come to tea.

I've seen the dog that loudly barks,
     I've chased a butterfly,
Watched robins, thrushes, even larks,
     And swallows in the sky.

Tiniest creatures, spiders, ants,
     Upon the ground I've seen:
Giraffes, gorillas, elephants,
     Upon the TV screen.

I watch the goldfish in our pool,
     As they swim to and fro:
Animals, humans, I've seen them all:
     No species I don't know.

Till last week when I discovered
     Species not known before:
Sometimes wrapped up well and covered
     And sometimes on the floor.

I jumped up to investigate
     And curled up by its head:
My people got into a state
     "Take off that cat," They said.

It had a kind of human head,
     But used no human talk:
Although it was a quadruped,
     I did not see it walk.

It did not talk in human words
      Or with a human sound:
Its scream was rather like a bird's
      That sees me on the ground.

They spoke to It with songs and hums,
      Not in their human style
But "Oohs" and "Ahs" and "Diddley Dums"
      And tried to make It smile.

Its body was not clothed in hair
      Like dog or pussy cat.
Sometimes it lay there quite, quite bare
      (And humans don't do that!)

One day they put It on a rug:
      It waved its legs about.
They picked It up to have a hug:
      It gave a happy shout.

It did not dig or use their loo
      (Excuse these words so frank),
It had a cloth to hold its pooh
      And - Ugh ! - it really stank.

It drank some milk - so that's Okay -
      This drink we cats prefer:
But did not lap the proper way
      And did not even purr.

Then when They said, "It's drunk enough"
      My folks were quite unkind,
Gave it a thump and pat so rough
      And said, "Bring up the wind."

To share my find I could not wait,
    But wanted some advice:
I went to see Old Tom my mate,
    For Tom is very wise.

Tom laughed - "I can explain it all.
    You are a full-grown Cat:
But once you were a Kitten small.
    Humans are just like that."

"This 'species strange' of which I hear
    Into a man will grow."
Human kitten? An odd idea!
    I suppose it could be so.

THE NEW COMPUTER or THE COMPUTER MOUSE

His new Computer comes today:
There's great excitement in the house.
"This new machine", I heard Him say,
"Will have a very special mouse."

It's here! - I watched - came by lorry -
I saw them eagerly unpack it:
Heard Her say: "I should be sorry
If anyone should try to hack it."
They took it to a space they'd cleared -
A little back room in our house.
I watched until at last appeared
A sight of a very special MOUSE.

They start to speak words new to cats -
HARDWARE and SOFT, CURSORS, ARGOL,
RAMS and ROMS, BITS, BUGS, FORMATS,
DISKETTES, some FLOPPY, and CABOL.
CP and UD TOO I HEARD -
Strange terms were uttered in our house:
I understood one single word
The mention of that special MOUSE.

Then I received religious shocks,
For C. of E. we've always been:
He's changed to Eastern Orthodox
And speaks of ICONS on a screen.
These things are puzzling to a cat:
I don't like changes in our house.
There is - disgust - a special MAT
Just for this very special MOUSE.

"It's USER-FRIENDLY", He had said,
"PROGRAMMES and DATA seem all right:
It's early yet to go to bed:
I'll try it out this very night."

I settled there without a sound -
That little back room of our house -
I watched Him tease it, move it round,
Playing with His special MOUSE.

When at long last He went to rest,
Eager, I pounced to eat my fill,
For mice I eat with joy and zest:
No mouse before has made me ill.

BUT-
Now in great pain upon the floor
My screams resound throughout the house:
I've never been so sick before
As when I ate that special MOUSE!

These two poems have an ecclesiastical flavour

MAGNIFICAT

Our Church's dedication!
    My folks will go along
To mark this great occasion
    With Festal Evensong.

"The Choir are celebrating -
    A fine MAGNIFICAT."
I crept inside, sat waiting
    To see a fine big cat.

I watched the Choir's keen faces,
    Singing with all their might -
Sopranos, Altos, Basses,
    But not a cat in sight.

A buxom Soprano seeking
    To reach a high B Flat
Made sounds like pussy squeaking -
    So that's MAGNIFICAT!

THE GOOD NEWS KATA CAT

Our Vicar sometimes comes to dine:
I listen while the People speak.
One day, while pouring out the wine,
The Vicar spoke some words in Greek.

"By Gospel our Good News is known:
In Greek it's Evangelion:
According to - by "kata" shown,
And so - by Mark - "kata Markon".

KATA! My word - used with Good News!
I do believe - no doubt of that!
I'll spread the Gospel or GOOD MEWS:
Evangelion kata Cat!

SOME MISUNDERSTANDINGS. We humans use several expressions about Cats. Our cat hears, but does not quite understand. The following verses show some of these -
Fat Cats, Catwalk, Raining Cats and Dogs.

FAT CATS

"Utilities when privatised -
Like Water, Gas" - They said
"Or trains or Phones (I was surprised)
Have FAT CATS at their head."

"The major Clearing Banks, whose costs
We folks cannot afford,"
My people moaned, "are also bossed
By FAT CATS on the Board."

With joy I heard and with elation!
Top Boards led by a CAT!
Old Tom could have some great relation
For Tom is wise and fat.

A Televised Meeting was planned
For all who held a Share,
I decided to watch this Cat so grand
In the Director's chair.

I watched at the time appointed
But sadly I turned away:
I saw and felt disappointed
A thin man dressed in grey.

CATWALK

Another time I heard Them talk
Of Fashions and Display:
A special place They call Catwalk,
I'm sure I heard Her say.

"Dresses for day and gowns for night:"
"The latest clothes just in"
"The wearers are a lovely sight" -
He added with a grin.

"We'll watch this show upon the box."
Up pricked my ears at that -
A Catwalk with some pretty frocks
Worn by a pretty cat.

With whiskers preened I settled down -
A naughty old voyeur! -
To see girl cats in evening gown,
Just right to start my purr.

But what is this??? Some human girls
Appeared all strangely dressed,
Some have straight hair, and some have curls:
My people seem impressed.

But I was NOT! Was this some trick?
I did not feel amused:
I give myself a thorough lick,
As always when confused.

Could I have got the message wrong ?
A Walk was there alright,
But only humans tripped along
With not a cat in sight!

RAINING CATS and DOGS

"It's raining Cats and Dogs!" She cried.
This gave me such a fright.
I rushed to the window to peer outside
And see this dreadful sight.

As I made this dash
I pictured in a flash -

Alsatians, Dalmatians,
Rotweilers, Retrievers, dignified Airedale
and Manx without tail,
Burmese, Siamese, Maltese, Balinese,
Poodles, Pugs, and Pekinese,
A Tabby looking scraggy,
And Moggies looking soggie,
Havana Brown falling down,
Through the air, Persian Longhair,
Afghan Hound hitting the ground,
Cats and dogs, black, coloured, white,
All mixed together - what a sight!

But when I peered through the window pane,
No awful sight I found:
All that I saw was the usual rain
And puddles on the ground.

And suddenly life became quite flat:
It had not rained one dog or cat.

CATTY REMARKS

Mrs Robinson is coming for a meal
And I can scarcely wait.
"Mrs Robinson - so what of that? Big Deal.
Is she your special mate?"

No - but I wait in eager anticipation
Because They said: "No doubt
She'll make catty remarks in her conversation
And have her claws right out."

I expect when she gossips about last week,
Telling her latest news,
"Catty remarks" means she'll use Pussy Cat Speak
With purrs and squeaks and mews.

What fun there'll be if things go really wrong!
Dinner will have more zest
If Mrs Robinson with claws sharp and long
Attacks another guest!

The great day came...She did not have sharp claws
But finger nails instead:
She kept them neat like our "Velvet Paws"
Though they were painted red.

With ears pricked up, I took in every word -
No mew or squeak or purr,
But "Mutton dressed like lamb"..."Guess what I heard."
"What does he see in her?"

"Helen in that coat looks an awful fright."
"Wasn't Anne's hair a mess?"
"Did you see the way those two behaved last night?"
"Sue thinks that Bill won't guess!"

22

"Dick's car was outside her house till two o'clock."
"Didn't Fred look shifty!"
"If I told all I know you'd get a shock."
"Jan is at least fifty."
"She had the cheek to call it Ministroni!"
"That awful cake Pat made!"
"I knew at once Val's boyfriend was a phoney."
"Her looks will quickly fade."

Much more like this: but no sharp claws appear:
No Catty Remarks I trace:
But only sounds and comments that I hear
From all the human race!

CRIME ...
CAT BURGLAR

Ther've been a lot of burglaries in our road this year:
I know about them since we had one here.
People have been talking and describing their loss,
Comparing notes and sounding very cross.
They reckon it must be the same person each time
For it was an identical method of crime.
He did not use an axe to smash a window pane
Or break the doors, force locks, but got in just the same.
Sometimes he climbed up drainpipes or along branches of trees:
Sometimes he used a small hole through which he could squeeze.
Then a rumour started which seemed beyond belief -
"A CAT BURGLAR," - all said - "must be this silent thief."

A BURGLAR CAT!
Just think of that!
I felt inside
A kind of pride,
And yet disgrace
For the feline race.

So I saw Old Tom for a chat
And told the news of Burglar Cat.
In view of human suspicion
We both felt we had a mission
To find who was the Burglar Cat,
Eliminating those too fat
For tiny holes or big tall trees:
We knew it could be none of these.
Those we thought we had detected
Went on our "List of Cats suspected" -
Roger was the foremost name
Of those who might be ones to blame.
Tabby who lived across the street
Was furtive and had nimble feet.

The Siamese might do some harm
Unless his squeak raised an alarm.
Blackie was very swift and slight:
His colour kept him hid at night.
Rufus, though getting old and staid,
When climbing walls was not afraid.
Ginger had a furtive face:
His wiry fur would leave no trace.
Fluffy could climb if she'd a mind:
But bits of fur would stick behind.
Bruiser, long famed for actions bold,
Would do it for the risks involved.

Those eight names plus a dozen more
Gave us a List of just a score.
Next move – their actions we'd espy
To see who had an alibi.

Bruiser on the relevant dates
Had been out drinking with his mates:
Fluffy dined with one of her beaux:
Rufus indoors with a cold in his nose:
Blackie was -

Before enquiries were complete
Exciting news ran through our street.
From house to house the message passed -
CAT BURGLAR has been caught at last!
Breaking in to Number Ten!
Old Tom and I were happy then,
But sorry we'd not had the time
To be the ones who solved the crime.
We did not know, but only guessed
Which of our cats was under arrest.
Caught in the act! So without fail
One of our cats would go to jail.

At last we heard: his name was BOB
"It must," Tom said, "be an Outside Job."
(To learn new terms Tom was not slow)
"Bob's not the name of a cat we know.
His photo's in the *'News'* tomorrow:
Is there a copy you could borrow?"
I borrowed the *'News'* for us to scan
And found - the photo of a Man!
Slight built, wiry, bit of a weed,
Yet not a Cat, a Man indeed.

"CAT BURGLAR"???

We did research both deep and wide,
Discovered what it signified.
At first we felt it some disgrace,
An insult to the feline race,
Yet pleased the saying had not meant
That any Pussy Cats were "Bent" -
Indeed it gave a certain thrill
To hear this tribute to our skill!

...and PUNISHMENT

CAT O' NINE TAILS
Some weeks after these burglaries took place
HE was holding forth one dinner time...
"This Crime Rate is a National Disgrace:
We're really getting far too soft on crime:
To control these villains we're quite unable:
Talking's no good: prison sentence fails.
"What we need" Big Thump on the table -
"Is to bring back the good old CAT O' NINE TAILS!"

At this I shook with fear and shivered -
He was in such an angry state -
Yet excited my tail stood up and quivered:
For cats could help reduce Crime Rate!
My TAIL. It is my proudest member:
Though I have ONE that's looking fine,
There must have been a time THEY can remember
When cats had seven, eight or NINE.

...Were those tails all at once erected
If some cause of happiness was found?
Or when their owner felt dejected
Did nine tails droop along the ground?
When their owner chased a leaf or feather
And life seemed very full of fun,
Did he waggle nine tails all together
Or wag them singly one by one?

The Children's Dictionary was illustrated.
I searched and found - but what a big surprise!
CAT O' NINE TAILS the caption clearly stated:
But the picture! I could scarce believe my eyes!

At first I thought it must have been a slip,
So carefully I checked the page again.
CAT O' NINE TAILS – "a savage kind of whip"
Which must have caused a very dreadful pain.

I suppose it's another human play on words,
But I will not make an awful fuss -
Except to ask - Why Cats? - not Dogs? – or Birds?
Or even Duck-billed Platypus?

27

EMPTY VESSELS MAKE THE MOST NOISE

"Empty vessels make the most noise"
So men and women, girls and boys
Must all be empty in their mind
Not full of thoughts like feline kind.

We cats are quiet all day long:
Only squeak if things go wrong:
A gentle purr shows life is sweet:
We always walk with padded feet.

Their day begins with noisy shock -
High-pitched scream from bedside clock.
We cats don't need to be so rough:
We wake up when we've slept enough.

"Children, wake up!" Father, mother,
Begin to shout at one another.
"Get dressed," "Come on," "It's ten to eight,"
"HURRY UP!" "YOU'LL ALL BE LATE!"

I peer outside: the weather's fine:
And stroll around till ten to nine.
Then creep inside: if no-one's there
I curl up in an easy chair.

But not for long! The 'phone is near:
A sudden ring right in my ear.
One of Her friends rings to chatter -
Half an hour of empty matter.

At last when I resume my sleep,
She thinks the carpet needs a sweep:
The Cleaner with its threatening roar
Makes an attack across the floor.

I escape on to a kitchen chair,
Happy to go on sleeping there:
The electric Mixer shrilly screams,
Disturbs my quiet feline dreams.

So it goes on, the ringing 'phone
Upsets my rest with bleeping tone:
Radio - Music - Talks - (such bores)
Support my mistress at her chores.

Disturbed by all these restless sounds,
I go outside, stroll through my grounds:
The weather's dry, but not too hot:
I curl up in my favourite spot...

A car door slams and He jumps out.
"I'm early back" I hear Him shout.
Then next there comes the dreaded cry -
"I'll cut the grass: the weather's dry."

Out comes the Monster I most fear:
Its dreadful growl is drawing near:
The noisy, threatening, whirling blade
Cuts grass that would give soothing shade.

Soon as this fearful task is done
The kids rush home all full of fun:
The final straw, the great disaster-
They've acquired a Ghetto Blaster!

Full minds would speak with softer voice,
Invent machines to make no noise.
These empty vessels make much sound:
WE CATS are full - of thoughts profound.

MANY HANDS MAKE LIGHT WORK

"Many hands can make light work" -
    One of their human "saws".
I'm not the kind of cat to shirk,
    So I gladly lend my paws.

Each day I help Her make the bed:
    I roll up in the sheet:
She plumped the pillow up: I said,
    "I'll press it with my feet."

When next She cooks some meat or fish,
    To give the guests a treat,
I have a lick at every dish
    To show it's fit to eat.

She then relaxes, does jigsaws,
    Puzzling to fit each bit:
To help I move each with my paws
    While on the board I sit.

Another way to help I find:
    When She does her knitting,
I help the ball of wool unwind
    Round where She is sitting.

Without my help She could not cope:
    I've made Her burden light:
Tomorrow I'll help again I hope
    After a restful night.

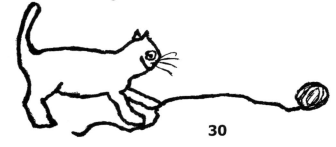

A CHANGE IS AS GOOD AS A REST
"A change is as good as a rest" -
        Their human sense of fun:
Our feline way is much the best -
        To change and rest in one.

I like to have a favourite space
        Where I can sit at ease.
Each month or so I change this place
        And find one that will please.

To suit one special kind of mood
        I choose a comfy chair:
If any stranger dare intrude,
        I fix him with a stare.

Then next I choose a site more flat,
        Where I can stretch out wide.
I stake my claim upon a mat,
        And folks must step aside.

Another time I choose a bed -
        "This pillow's clean, I hope,
And soft enough to rest my head".
        If that door's shut, I mope.

Another month, another chair:
        All else is second-best.
This is *my* spot: let no-one dare
        To fill my place of rest.

She brings a box back from the shop,
        Full of the things She's bought:
It's emptied out: inside I hop:
        Pretend it is my fort.

Why do I change? My bits of fur
        Show a need for cleaning?
Or just a whim? Or my own smell?
        There must be *some* deep meaning!

THERE'S NOWT SO QUEER AS FOLKS

"There's nowt so queer as folks indeed,"
    I heard some humans say:
With this we Pussy Cats agreed:
    Just take last Christmas Day...

The folks had talked of shopping sprees
    With cash or credit card.
One and all, they longed to please
    And tried so very hard.

When Christmas came, I watched to learn
    What all this bustle meant –
Each one received and gave in turn
    A thing they called "Present."

Then next the folks these things untied,
    Each adult, girl and boy:
And when they saw the things inside,
    Gave little squeals of joy.

"I really, really wanted this."
    "It fits me just a treat."
"Come here and have a thank you kiss."
    "You are a perfect sweet."

"This present must have cost the earth."
    "A wonderful surprise."
(Catlike I watched with silent mirth,
    For some were telling lies.)

So this is what it's all about –
    They give to show they care:
I did not want to be left out,
    So found the choicest fare.

I waited long outside the house –
    Then pounced - so sharp! - so swift!
And caught a lovely, tasty mouse:
    The very perfect gift.

" 'twill give the one I love a treat."
    I went with happy purr
And laid it right beside Her feet,
    A special gift for Her.

She gave a squeal, but not of joy,
    Her wrath she did not hide:
"You are a messy little boy –
    Just take that thing outside!"

To catch that mouse cost half my day:
    I wanted it myself.
"There's nowt so queer as folks," they say:
    She'd said those word Herself.

O.K. I'd eaten half the head:
    But why make such a fuss?
"There's nowt so queer as folks" - well said:
    Not sensible like us!

33

LAUGHTER IS THE BEST MEDICINE

Have you ever tried to give a pill or other medicine to a cat?
If so, you will appreciate this poem.
What we see as an exasperating task is a source of amusement to
the cat.

My ears are sharp and up they prick
    When those true words are said.
I proved they're true last week when sick
    And really feeling dead...

"Did you see him, shaking, shiver?
    He's had no food at all:
Could be infection of the liver,
    Perhaps a big fur ball.

Tomorrow we'll take him to the Vet,
    Who'll see what's wrong inside."
The following day She went to get
    That box in which I ride.

I'm claustrophobic when confined,
    So used a feline wile:
Hid where it took Her hours to find
    And gave a secret smile.

The Vet with needle sharp drew near:
    "Let's see if this will work."
"You'll have to catch me first, I fear,"
    I thought with inner smirk.

"Your cat can scratch although he's ill!
    Mixed with some food or drink
Three times a day give him this pill."
    I thought, "That's what you think".

A tasty meal they cooked that night.
   I saw what they had done -
They hid that pill right out of sight.
   I thought: "Let's have some fun."

Made out I did not know their trick:
   Ate all that tasty fish:
I grinned, then had a final lick -
   The pill stayed in the dish!

He wrapped a towel round my claws:
   My mouth She opened wide,
And holding my reluctant jaws,
   That pill she popped inside.

Gentle but firm, my neck She stroked,
   And thought She'd won the day:
I spat it out (I'd nearly choked!)
   And grinning ran away.

I escaped as She ran after,
   My hidey-hole I found:
I shivered, shook - but with laughter -
   And felt quite fit and sound!

LAUGHTER OF MEDICINES IS THE BEST.
   I think you will agree -
Although my folk became distressed,
   That treatment worked for me!

DON'T LET THE CAT OUT OF THE BAG

"She'll let the cat out of the bag."
    They whispered together.
Laughing, She said: "We'll need a gag!"
    This made me wonder whether -

Was I the Pussy Cat they meant
    To imprison in a sack?
To lie there with my legs all bent,
    Little space to stretch my back.

Not able to chase the birds or mice,
    Feel the warmth of summer sun.
This punishment was far from nice:
    I considered crimes I'd done...

... Sometimes not acting as I should
    Sitting docile on my mat:
I think I'm neither *very* good
    Nor a *very* wicked cat.

Their words gave me a dreadful fright.
    Off I crept without a sound
To hide myself right out of sight
    In a hidey-hole I'd found.

I asked Old Tom, who has good sense,
    "Help me in my deep disgrace:
Will you be Counsel for Defence,
    Plead for me and state my case?"

Old Tom replied: "Don't be afraid:
    It's what they call Id-i-om:
It means a secret is betrayed."
    Heartily I thanked Old Tom.

I walked back home with legs quite free,
    Felt the sunshine on my back,
Sharpened my claws upon a tree.
    No fear now of bag or sack!

Our little cat now ventures into the learned realms of Philosophy and Psychology with COGITO ERGO SUM and OEDIPUS COMPLEX. He does not, however, get things quite right...

COGITO ERGO SUM

"COGITO ERGO SUM" - I read the words myself
When I had a look
In a big fat book
Which the master forgot to replace on the shelf.

I was puzzled by this, though ashamed to state it,
For cats never show
That they do not know.
So I asked OLD TOM next door to translate it.

He was puzzled at first: "We won't let it floor us."
Old Tom was well read
With brains in his head:
"We need reference books, dictionary, Thesaurus".

He put piles of books by the chair that he sat in:
We had a long read,
Then found what we need.
"Cogito ergo sum" - the language was Latin!

"Of course I knew all the time," Tom said with a wink.
Eager I waited
Till Tom translated:
"I think and so I am." "I am because I think."

"It comes back to me now: it's a thing I once heard,"
Said Tom with a start:
"It comes from Descartes –
Descartes means 'of cats,' it's a foreign French word".

"Cartesian is a philosophical style."
It seemed like ages –
Both scanned the pages:
"I suppose it means cats," said Tom with a smile.

We sat in silence then, pondering what was taught
By SUM.......   COGNITO....
I Exist.....   I know.....
For Cats can spend long hours wrapt in silent thought.

How happy we both felt that day we'd not have missed!
Tails high in the air!
Cartesian pair:
Old Tom and I both live: we think, so we exist!

OEDIPUS COMPLEX

Young Peter next door is a very nice lad,
      But different from his brother:
He looks rather strange and sometimes quite sad,
      He seems over fond of his mother.

If she's at home he stays by her side
      And never goes out with another:
He never goes out for a walk or a ride
      Unless escorting his mother.

He never goes out for a drink with the boys:
      Though thirty he's not had a lover:
He's like a small child at home with his toys
      And happy to stay with his mother.

His family thought of the life that he missed
      And made a terrible fuss:
They brought in a man called Psychologist -
      "COMPLEX," I heard: "EEDIE PUSS."

"Now Peter" I thought "Won't be sad any more:
      They've found why he's lonely and needy
And I'm so glad we'll have living next door
      A girl Pussy called Edith or Eedie."

THERE ARE MORE WAYS THAN ONE TO KILL A CAT

He had a business friend called Joe
    Who sometimes came and dined,
And one day said, "You ought to know
    I've something on my mind."

"There's a decision I must make
    Before this week is done:
I do not know which course to take:
    Which is the proper one?"

They spoke strange words of Interest Earned,
    Of Money, Stocks and Shares:
And then to animals they turned
    And spoke of Bulls and Bears.

"We can do this ... we might do that ...
    We must this problem solve.
MORE WAYS THAN ONE TO KILL A CAT:
    Let's act with firm resolve.
A drastic action we must dare -
    Follow the boldest way."
In fear I hid behind a chair
    And stayed there all that day.

After this shock, our little cat reverts to more intellectual pursuits and tries his skill at writing TWO SONNETS, followed by some EPIGRAMS. This is not easy...

My dears, the trouble that I took
Looking up SONNET in Her book!
It said "Ten Silly Bulls"(?) Indeed!
But that is what each line must need.
Just fourteen lines, and that's a fact -
Not one too short or one too long.
The Rhyming Scheme must be exact:
The Scansion too must not go wrong.
A hard task for a CAT you know,
But here they are: I've had a go!

40

CAT WORDS: A SONNET

She was doing the Crossword yesterday,
Dictionary left just where She sat.
I found some new words I'd not heard them say
When I studied my special entry CAT.
For combing our fur there's a CATacomb,
CATalogue thrown on a cosy log fire.
(Tom later said one's a kind of tomb,
The other's a list to help the buyer.)
There's a CATamaran that sails on the sea.
Strophe I know is a kind of a verse:
Of course a Cat's poem – CATastophe!
But Tom's explained it's something much worse.
Difficult words – like CATarrh, CATalyst,
Tom will explain – he's a good CATechist.

CLEANLINESS IS NEXT TO GODLINESS: A SONNET

"Cleanliness is next to Godliness."
How true for cats! We cannot stand a mess.
The slightest smell lingering in earth tray
Will make us turn, disgusted, walk away.
Should dirty mark be seen upon our dish
We will refuse to eat the freshest fish.
At least six times a day we have a lick.
We rush to hide if we are feeling sick.
Embarrassed by Faux Pas we don't go red,
But – nonchalant – we have a wash instead.
When nature calls, holes we dig for faeces
And bury them (not like some other species!).
If cleanliness is next to Godliness indeed
We Pussies are a very pious breed.

Old Tom explained the meaning of Bull in the two poems on the facing page and solved the confusion between Silly Bulls and Syllables.

CAT'S EPIGRAMS

"HIS BARK," They say "IS MUCH WORSE THAN HIS BITE."
Well,...O.K. then... this proverb may be right.
Next door's Alsatian barks: I do not pause
To make a detailed study of his jaws.

"IT'S ENOUGH TO MAKE A CAT LAUGH," they state
When some fellow human's folly they relate.
This implies we cats of solemn mind
Lack humour in our head.
A good laugh we have at human kind
When they're tucked up in bed.

"LOOK BEFORE YOU LEAP" may be all right
For man,
Who cannot leap five times his height
And land
On a table full of things out of sight.
Cats can.

"A BIRD IN HAND IS WORTH TWO IN THE BUSH,"
They say, but I don't believe that:
When I held in my paws a lovely fat thrush,
They say, "You cruel, wicked cat."

"A CAT MAY LOOK AT A KING." Indeed!
Of course he certainly can.
We cats are a very superior breed,
While a king is only a man.

CATMINT
"I've bought some Catmint for that empty space."
I had wondered what she meant.
Though the flower was not like a Pussy Cat's face,
I went quite mad at the scent!

TAILPIECE

"CATS HAVE NINE LIVES," one day I heard.
Never was said a truer word.
Dear Reader, now my verse you've read
You know th'adventurous life I've led.
THE BURGLARS who ransacked our house:
The night I ate COMPUTER MOUSE:
The day when I, though taken ill,
Was cured by LAUGHTER, not their pill.
To KILL A CAT gave me a fear
That my own death might soon be near.
OUT OF THE BAG THE CAT SHE'LL LET
Gave me another cause to fret.
That takes me up to Number FOUR:
Mistakes I've made increase the score.
With EIGHT lives gone I have deserved
That Number NINE shall be preserved.
From now I'll cultivate my mind,
Write Sonnets, Odes, if so inclined
And so, dear Reader, I retire
To curl up safe beside the fire.